Peekaboo baby
どーこだ

Sujatha Lalgudi

どーこだ?　－こどものほん

Author/Illustrator: Sujatha Lalgudi

Translation: まつお　やえ　やく

This book Belongs to:

—————————————————————

Where are Baby's Eyes?

おめめは　どこだ?

Here they are, two twinkling eyes.

ここだよぱっちり　おめめが　ふたつ

Where is the baby's nose?

あれ　あれ?

おはなは　どーこだ?

Here it is, one shiny nose.

ちっちゃな　おはな　みいつけた！

Where is the baby's mouth?

おくちが　ないぞ?

Here it is, rosy lips.

かわいい　おくちが　かくれんぼ

Where are the baby's ears?

おみみは　どこにあるのかなぁ?

Here they are, two ears
that hear.

あった　あった
よく　きこえるよ

Where are the baby's fingers?
ゆびは　　どこだろう?

Here they are, ten lovely fingers.
ほーら かわいい　ゆびが　10ぽん！

Where are the baby's toes?

あしが　みえないなぁ...

Here they are, ten tiny toes.

でてきた　でてきた
あしのゆびも　10ぽん！

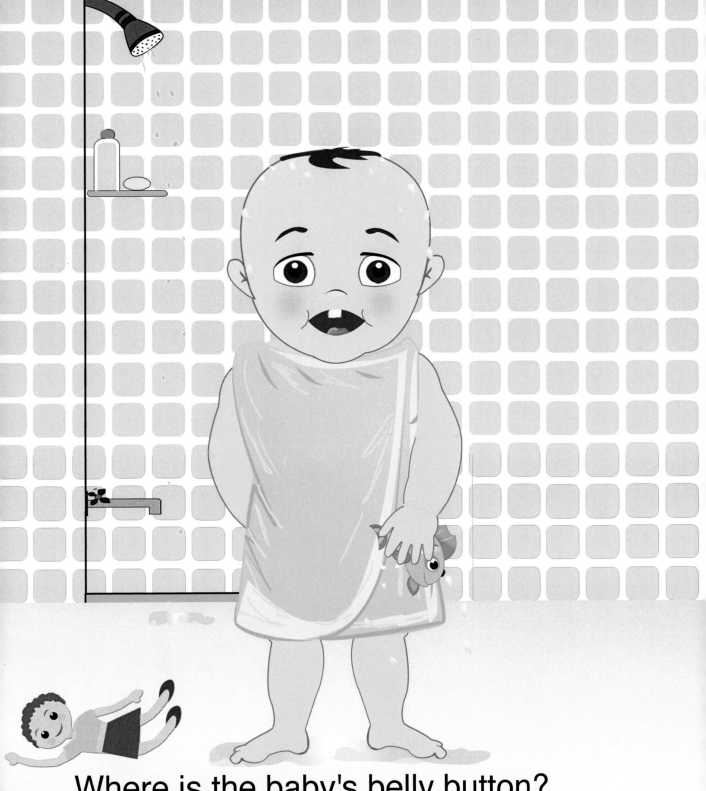

Where is the baby's belly button?

おへそは　どこに　あるのかな?

Here it is!

ここだよー

Where is the baby?

あかちゃんは　どこだ?

Here I am!

ここにいるよ！

Peekaboo

どーこだ

We could read a book.

ふうっと　ひといき
じゅんびかんりょう

Finish your milk, sleepy baby.

さぁ　ミルクを
のんだら
ねるじかん...

Good Night. Sweet Dreams Baby!

おやすみなさい
いいゆめ　みてね

Hope you enjoyed reading this book
to your child.
Please write a kind review if you did.
Thank you.

Sujatha Lalgudi

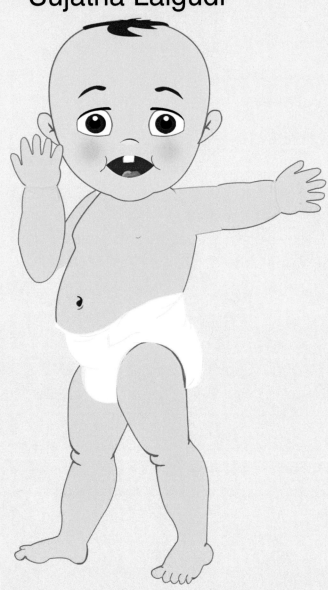

The End